RECONSTRUCTING AMERICA

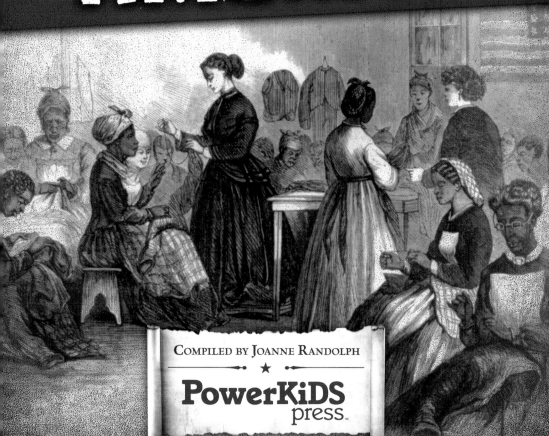

COMPILED BY JOANNE RANDOLPH

PowerKiDS
press™

Published in 2018 by The Rosen Publishing Group, Inc.
29 East 21st Street, New York, NY 10010

Race Relations by Andrew Matthews from Cobblestone Magazine (December 2006)
Reconstructing America by Craig E. Blohm from Cobblestone Magazine (February 2001)
Weighing in on Civil Rights by Ruth Tenzer Feldman from Cobblestone Magazine (January 2003)

Cataloging-in-Publication Data

Names: Randolph, Joanne.
Title: Reconstructing America / compiled by Joanne Randolph.
Description: New York : PowerKids Press, 2018. | Series: The Civil War and Reconstruction: rebellion and rebuilding | Includes glossary and index.
Identifiers: LCCN ISBN 9781538340981 (pbk.) | ISBN 9781538340974 (library bound) | ISBN 9781538340998 (6 pack)
Subjects: LCSH: Reconstruction (U.S. history, 1865-1877)--Juvenile literature. | United States--History--Civil War, 1861-1865--Juvenile literature.
Classification: LCC E668.R436 2018 | DDC 973.7--dc23

Designer: Katelyn E. Reynolds
Editor: Joanne Randolph

Photo credits: Cvr, pp. 1, 5, 6, 8, 12, 13, 14 (all), 17, 19 courtesy of the Library of Congress; cvr, pp. 1–32 (background texture) javarman/Shutterstock.com; cvr, pp. 1–32 (flags) cybrain/Shutterstock.com; cvr, pp. 1–32 (scroll) Seregam/Shutterstock.com; p. 10 Art and Picture Collection, The New York Public Library. "Freedmen Voting In New Orleans." New York Public Library Digital Collections. Accessed February 2, 2018. http://digitalcollections.nypl.org/items/510d47e1-3fd9-a3d9-e040-e00a18064a99; p. 19 Artindo/Shutterstock.com; p. 21 -/AFP/Getty Images; p. 22 Poet Sage Photos/Shutterstock.com; p. 24 Carl Iwasaki/The LIFE Images Collection/Getty Images; p. 26 Tom/Wikipedia.org (http://photolab.lbjlib.utexas.edu/detail.asp?id=18031); p. 29 a katz/Shutterstock.com

Manufactured in the United States of America

CPSIA Compliance Information: Batch #CS18PK: For Further Information contact Rosen Publishing, New York, New York at 1-800-237-9932

CONTENTS

WORDS IN THE GLOSSARY APPEAR
IN **BOLD** TYPE THE FIRST TIME
THEY ARE USED IN THE TEXT.
★

RECONSTRUCTING AMERICA

Even before the Civil War ended, President Abraham Lincoln had begun to consider how the Confederate states should be received back into the Union.

Conceived in 1863, his Reconstruction plan was remarkably **lenient**. Lincoln decided that if ten percent of the voters in a Confederate state signed an oath of loyalty to the United States, that state would be readmitted to the Union. He also tentatively wanted to give the newly freed blacks the right to vote. But, Lincoln's plans were met with some resistance. A group of congressmen, known as the **Radical** Republicans, wanted to punish the states that had seceded. Lincoln disagreed with the Radical Republicans' agenda and opposed their **legislation**. He felt putting the Union back together was more important than punishing the South.

THIS PHOTOGRAPH OF PRESIDENT LINCOLN WAS TAKEN ON AUGUST 9, 1863, WHILE THE COUNTRY WAS STILL EMBROILED IN CIVIL WAR.

5

ANDREW JOHNSON SERVED AS
THE NATION'S SEVENTEENTH PRESIDENT
FROM 1865 TO 1869.

★

6

Then, in 1865, Lincoln was assassinated. His vice president, Andrew Johnson, became head of the country. The Radical Republicans thought the new president would be on their side.

But Johnson had his own ideas about Reconstruction. His Reconstruction plan would grant a pardon to Southerners who signed a loyalty oath. Southern states then would be allowed to form new governments and petition for readmission to the Union. He also said that all lands the Union had seized and distributed to freed slaves during the war would revert back to the original owners. The Radical Republicans were not satisfied with giving the South back so much or allowing it to rebuild state governments without federal oversight and intervention.

When Congress convened in the fall of 1865, however, the Radical Republicans prevented former Confederate congressmen from taking their seats. So, the Southerners vowed to come up with their own Reconstruction plan. While politicians fought it out in Washington, D.C., Southern whites and African Americans faced more immediate problems.

This photograph, taken in april 1865, shows Richmond, Virginia, in ruins.

During the Civil War, Southern cities had been destroyed and rural areas turned into what one journalist described as "a broad black streak of ruin and desolation." Besides the physical destruction, the war and its aftermath also took a psychological toll on the Southern white population. First, the South was humiliated by its defeat. Then, Northerners started to travel south to enforce Reconstruction. In addition, African Americans began to take part in Southern legislatures. Black churches flourished, providing a sense of community for the newly **emancipated** African Americans. In December 1865, the Thirteenth **Amendment** to the U.S. Constitution was ratified, officially ending slavery.

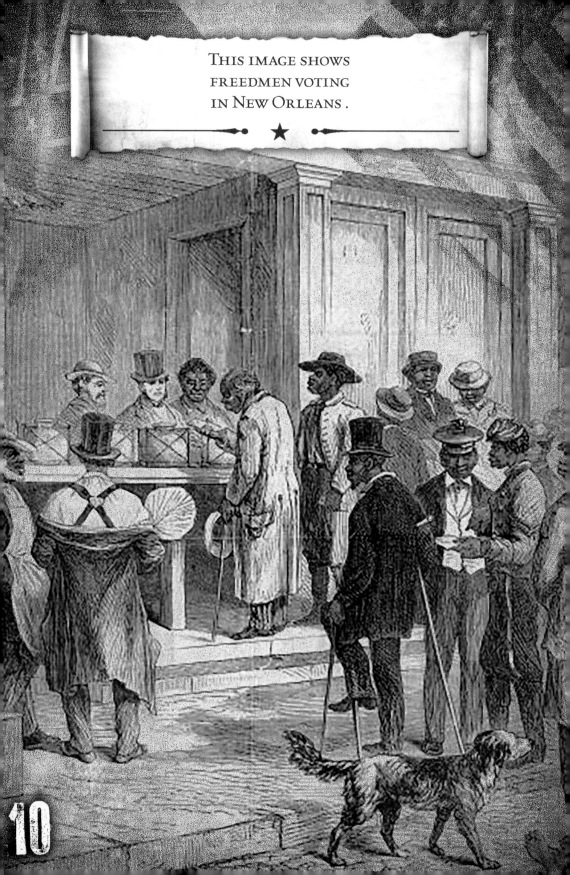

THIS IMAGE SHOWS FREEDMEN VOTING IN NEW ORLEANS.

Although African Americans were legally free, Southern whites did not automatically welcome them as full citizens. To control the new freedmen, the Southern states passed legislation called Black Codes. These laws gave African Americans some freedom, such as the right to own property, but restricted them in many more ways. Free black people could not own firearms or assemble in groups. They could not serve on juries. Under the codes, African Americans without jobs could be arrested for **vagrancy**. Often, they were forced to sign long contracts with employers for little pay. Many black people were restricted to doing fieldwork or household labor. In reality, they were little better off than they had been as slaves.

Congress soon realized that only by adding to the Constitution could black people be assured of their rights. The Fourteenth and Fifteenth Amendments were ratified in 1868 and 1870, respectively. These gave African Americans equal protection under the law and prohibited discrimination in voting due to race. (Voting discrimination due to gender was still encountered, however: Women would not gain the right to vote until 1920.) But, despite some constitutional equality, African Americans still faced unfair treatment that often threatened their lives.

This article appeared in *Harper's Weekly* in 1866. It depicts scenes in Memphis, Tennessee, during the riot there.

★

HARPER'S WEEKLY.

A JOURNAL OF CIVILIZATION.

VOL. X.—No. 491.]　　NEW YORK, SATURDAY, MAY 26, 1866.　　SINGLE COPIES TEN CENTS.
$4.00 PER YEAR IN ADVANCE.

Entered according to Act of Congress, in the Year 1866, by Harper & Brothers, in the Clerk's Office of the District Court for the Southern District of New York.

THE MEMPHIS RIOTS.

There was in Memphis, on the first two days of May, an excitement unequaled since the close of the war. The origin of the disturbance between the whites and negroes of that city was highly discreditable to the colored soldiers, and the riotous proceedings which followed were a disgrace to civilization. For the riot the lower class of white citizens were as responsible as were the soldiers of the Third United States Colored Infantry for the original difficulty. This regiment, whose reputation has been a bad one, had been mustered out, since which they had frequented whisky-shops in the southern part of the city, and had been guilty of excesses and disorderly conduct. On the evening of May 1 come drunken members of the regiment were on South Street, talking loudly, when in an insolent manner they were ordered by two policemen to cease their noise and disperse. Words ensued, followed by blows, throwing of missiles, and firing of revolvers.

To understand what followed it must be remembered that the police force of Memphis is composed mostly of Irishmen, whose violent prejudice against negroes was so shamefully displayed in the New York riots of 1863. The *Times* correspondent thus describes the riot:

Word was sent to police head-quarters, and the whole force at once proceeded to the scene of the fray, being joined on the way thither by a loud and excited citizens. Meanwhile the firing had brought out other negroes to the spot, some armed with clubs and come with revolvers, so that by the time the police force came up the two parties were about equal in number. The negroes held the original

position, out, upon the approach of the police, showing no determination to abandon it, were fired upon by the police and citizens who accompanied them. This fire was returned, and for a while both parties busied themselves in discharging their revolvers as rapidly as possible. Meanwhile word was sent to General Runyons, who promptly disputched to the scene of action a company of Regulars (which), when the negroes were quickly dispersed and driven in every direction.

During the evening the wildest and most exaggerated reports soon spread throughout the city. Every conceivable outrage of the intelligence of the fight told a different story, and the highest excitement prevailed. Each report placed a worse aspect upon the affair than the preceding one, and only served to develop the pent-up prejudices against the negro. Soon after dark this excitement and population flamed out. Large numbers of armed citizens repaired to the scene of the fight and commenced firing upon every negro who made himself visible. One negro upon South Street, a quiet, inoffensive laborer, was shot down almost in front of his own cabin, and after life was extinct his body was fired into, and beat in a most horrible manner. In all parts of the city, wherever they could be seen, negroes were fired upon by policemen as well as citizens. They were shot while driving hacks, and quietly walking in the streets about their business. The police seemed to make it their special business to shoot every negro they could see, no matter where he was or what he was doing. The result was that by 9 o'clock the excited people were indiscriminately firing at old ones. How many negroes were killed during the night it is impossible to ascertain, or to say was conveniently tough during the darkness, for the hours in all parts of the city. It is estimated that from 15 to 20 were killed. So far as I have been able to learn, not a white man was fired upon by a negro during the whole night.

After the fight of Tuesday evening the negro soldiers and most of the colored population residing in the vicinity of the fight fled to the fort for security. They were perfectly quiet—in fact, were terribly frightened for their own safety. At an early hour yesterday morning every thing

SCENES IN MEMPHIS, TENNESSEE, DURING THE RIOT—BURNING A FREEDMEN'S SCHOOL-HOUSE.

[Sketched by A. R. W.]

SCENES IN MEMPHIS, TENNESSEE, DURING THE RIOT—SHOOTING DOWN NEGROES ON THE MORNING OF MAY 2, 1866.—[Sketched by A. R. W.]

In 1866, riots between African Americans and whites broke out in Memphis, Tennessee, and New Orleans, Louisiana, leaving nearly 100 black people dead or injured. Beginning in 1865, night horsemen wearing white robes and hoods could be seen throughout the South. Called the Ku Klux Klan (KKK), this secret organization's main goal was to prevent black people from voting. It accomplished this by terrorizing African Americans with threats and physical violence. Lynchings, beatings, and shootings of black people and their white sympathizers became frequent occurrences in the South during the Reconstruction era.

KU KLUX KLAN MEMBERS

EXAMPLES OF SEPARATE FACILITIES
FOR BLACKS AND WHITES
COULD BE FOUND ALL ACROSS THE SOUTH.

When Reconstruction ended in 1877, any strides black citizens had made ended with it. The 1880s and 1890s saw the enactment of "Jim Crow" laws, which further **discriminated** against African Americans. Named for a minstrel show character, these laws fostered the separation of the races in trains, streetcars, restaurants, parks, schools, and other public places. In 1896, the U.S. Supreme Court upheld the legality of "separate but equal" facilities, even though those for black people usually were inferior.

African Americans no longer were slaves, but were they truly free? A revealing answer came from future president James Garfield. "What is freedom?" Garfield asked in 1865. "Is it the bare privilege of not being chained? If this is all, then freedom is a bitter mockery, a cruel delusion." Only through the work of activists such as Ida B. Wells would this delusion eventually begin to give way to real freedom.

RACE RELATIONS

After the Civil War, the South refused to support the civil rights amendments of the 1860s and 1870s that guaranteed freedoms to African Americans. Acts of terror increased against newly freed slaves and other black Americans in the South. The Ku Klux Klan continued to use fear and violence to prevent black southerners from exercising their political rights.

Ulysses S. Grant may not have been a true **abolitionist**, but he believed that black people deserved fair treatment and was determined to use his presidential authority to uphold the nation's laws. Between 1870 and 1871, his administration introduced laws called the Enforcement Acts. Specifically aimed at the KKK, these laws made it illegal to interfere with African American men who were practicing their newly acquired political freedoms, such as voting, holding office, or registering to vote.

Ulysses S. Grant had gained fame as a general in the U.S. Army during the Civil War. He served as the nation's eighteenth president from 1869 to 1877.

UNITED
STATES

SANTO
DOMINGO

Grant also proposed **annexing** Santo Domingo (present-day Dominican Republic). He believed it could become a place to which **persecuted** southern blacks could relocate. Grant reasoned that if white landowners thought African Americans had somewhere else to go, they would treat black people better and pay them more to stay and work on the **plantations**. This idea did not get a lot of support.

Grant ultimately lacked the ability to solve the nation's difficult race relations problems. Once, when white citizens tried to forcibly unseat fairly elected black politicians in Louisiana, Grant sent the army to restore order. This act of force only served to enrage southerners more, however, as well as alarm some northerners.

By 1873, a financial panic and the economic **depression** that followed became the most important issue for Americans. Nearly 100 years would pass before the nation again focused on civil rights and attempted to finish what had been started at the end of the Civil War.

SANTO DOMINGO, 1871

AFTER RECONSTRUCTION

With a large amount of **prejudice** remaining after the Civil War and Reconstruction Era, most African Americans made little headway politically or economically. Jim Crow laws in the South made it illegal for African Americans and whites to use the same facilities, be it public transportation, schools, churches, or restaurants. But in the 1950s and 1960s, a few brave leaders began to push for a better life for African Americans.

The civil rights movement of the 1950s and 1960s didn't solve the problems of African Americans overnight, though. It created new issues regarding the balance of power among the three branches of government. In those decades of tremendous social change, the federal government rarely spoke with one united voice. Different branches took the lead in promoting change at different times. Sometimes the various arms helped the progress of civil rights, and sometimes they did not.

CIVIL RIGHTS LEADER MARTIN LUTHER KING JR.
ADDRESSES SUPPORTERS
ON AUGUST 28, 1963, DURING
THE FAMOUS "MARCH ON WASHINGTON."

THE SUPREME COURT BUILDING
IS LOCATED
IN WASHINGTON, D.C.

22

After the Civil War (1861–1865), the Thirteenth, Fourteenth, and Fifteenth amendments to the Constitution were passed. These amendments provided former slaves with the rights of citizenship previously denied to them. The states, and later the federal government, however, found ways to interpret the laws so that discrimination against African Americans continued to exist.

The Supreme Court was the first arm of the federal government to further define the rights of black Americans. This does not mean that the Supreme Court has always supported the rights of minorities in the United States. There have been times when the Court's decisions have reflected the views held by the people governing the nation. But times change and so do Supreme Court justices. This was particularly true in the 1950s when the Court began to rule in favor of racial equality.

But Congress was not yet willing to legislate according to the Court's decisions. For example, shortly after World War II, the law school at the University of Texas refused to admit Heman Sweatt, a black veteran. Instead, the university established a separate law school for him to attend. Sweatt challenged this action in court. In 1950, basing the decision on its interpretation of the Constitution, the Supreme Court ordered the university to admit Sweatt to its regular law school.

This photograph shows the students and parents who initiated the landmark case *Brown v. Board of Education of Topeka, Kansas.*

One of the Supreme Court's most famous decisions, which struck down **segregated** schools, came in 1954 with *Brown v. Board of Education of Topeka, Kansas*. The case involved schoolchildren from districts that permitted or required separate schools for African Americans. In the Topeka district, the schools for black children were far inferior to those attended by white children. The Court determined that separate was not equal in this case.

Between 1955 and 1969, many things happened in the civil rights arena. Segregation laws and states' rights became **hot button** issues for many Americans. Who had the final say in interpreting the laws of the nation? The people and state governments in some areas of the South did not want the federal government interfering with their local authority. Americans on both sides of the argument took to the streets to express their views.

There were several instances when the executive branch became swept up in the movement for civil rights. In 1957, the governor of Arkansas tried to prevent nine black students from attending the all-white Central High School in Little Rock. He called in that state's **National Guard**. But President Dwight D. Eisenhower was determined to uphold the *Brown v. Board of Education of Topeka, Kansas* decision. He sent U.S. Army soldiers to Little Rock with orders to protect the nine African American teenagers.

MARTIN LUTHER KING JR. LOOKS ON AS PRESIDENT LYNDON B. JOHNSON SIGNS THE CIVIL RIGHTS ACT OF 1964 INTO LAW.

Another case of presidential intervention occurred in 1962. President John F. Kennedy ordered federal marshals to escort a young black man, James Meredith, to class at the University of Mississippi. When rioting threatened the safety of Meredith and the marshals, Kennedy sent 16,000 troops to protect them and control the mob. Federal troops remained at the university until Meredith graduated a year later.

As more and more people expressed their desire for laws that ended racial discrimination, elected officials in Congress took the lead by passing the Civil Rights Act of 1964, the Voting Rights Act of 1965, and the Civil Rights Act of 1968. The 1964 act, pushed through Congress by President Lyndon B. Johnson, has proven to be one of the most significant pieces of civil rights legislation to date.

One provision of that act guarantees equal access to public places for people of all races. Lester Maddox, owner of a whites-only restaurant in Georgia, challenged this in the Supreme Court. The justices ruled against him, stating that Congress had the power to regulate accommodations to travelers under the Constitution's interstate commerce clause. Similarly, in the Voting Rights Act, Congress provided that federal inspectors had the right to observe voter registration, as well as state and county elections.

South Carolina sued in the Supreme Court to prevent these inspections, claiming that the law infringed on states' rights under the Constitution. The Court ruled that, under the Fifteenth Amendment, Congress had acted properly by protecting the right of citizens to vote without regard to race. Sometimes the different branches of the federal government obstructed the progress of civil rights in America. Yet, in the twentieth century, it took all three arms to advance the movement and to work for and achieve equal rights for all American citizens.

Though Reconstruction officially ended in 1877, it took a century for African Americans to truly make headway in gaining equal rights, finally seeing some results during the 1950s and 1960s. Even so, there is still a long way to go before all Americans can claim true equality. Some people continue to hold prejudices against difference, but Americans across the country are working hard every day to improve life for all people.

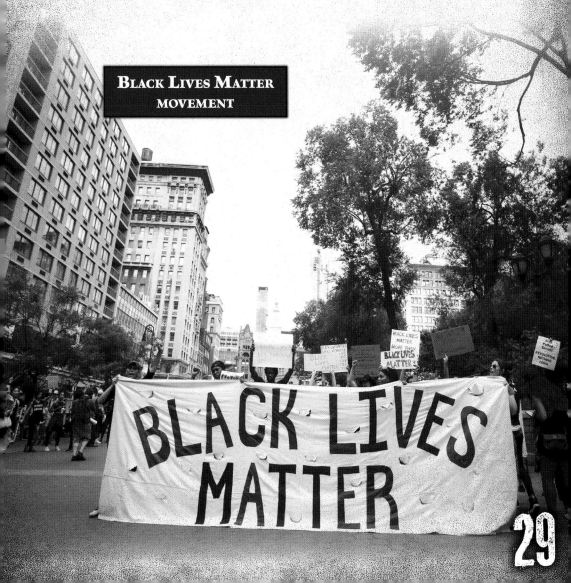

BLACK LIVES MATTER
MOVEMENT

GLOSSARY

abolitionist: Someone who wants to do away with something they believe is harmful to society, such as slavery.

amendment: A change or addition to a legal document or to the U.S. Constitution.

annexing: Adding land to one's territory.

depression: A long and severe recession in an economy or market.

discriminate: To treat a person or a group of people badly because of who they are, typically based on race, gender, religion, or other things.

emancipated: Freed.

hot button: A tendency for an issue to gain an immediate, highly emotional response.

legislation: Proposed laws.

lenient: Merciful or not harsh.

National Guard: The military reserve units that are controlled by individual states, equipped by the federal government, and subject to be called on by either.

persecuted: Treated someone badly because of their race, religion, political beliefs, gender, or other reasons.

plantation: An estate on which crops such as tobacco, sugar, and coffee are grown by resident workers.

prejudice: Dislike, hostility, or unfair treatments based on unfounded opinions that are not based on reason or real experience.

radical: Having to do with complete political or social change.

segregate: To separate people by enforcing unfair laws that keep them apart. Segregation is usually based on race.

vagrancy: A state of being without a permanent home or job.

FOR MORE INFORMATION

BOOKS

Latta, Susan. *Reconstruction Era*. Minneapolis, MN: Core Library, 2014.

Marsico, Katie. *The Reconstruction Era*. Vero Beach, FL: Rourke Educational Media, 2013.

WEBSITES

Reconstruction
http://www.history.com/topics/american-civil-war/reconstruction

Tracing Center: Reconstruction, Jim Crow, and the Civil Rights Era
http://www.tracingcenter.org/resources/background/reconstruction-jim-crow-and-the-civil-rights-era/

INDEX